How Shall We Travel?

Helen Lanz

SEA-TO-SEA

Mankato Collingwood London

This edition first published in 2012 by

Sea-to-Sea Publications
Distributed by Black Rabbit Books
P.O. Box 3263, Mankato, Minnesota 56002

Printed in China

9 8 7 6 5 4 3 2

Published by arrangement with the Watts
Publishing Group Ltd, London.

Library of Congress Cataloging-in-Publication Data

Lanz, Helen.
 How shall we travel / by Helen Lanz.
     p. cm. -- (Go green)
 Includes index.
 ISBN 978-1-59771-302-3 (library binding)
 1. Travel--Environmental aspects--Juvenile literature. 2. Transportation--
Environmental aspects--Juvenile literature. 3. Transportation--Energy
conservation--Juvenile literature. I. Title.
 G156.5.E58L36 2012
 388--dc22
                              2011005451

Series Editor: Julia Bird
Design: D.R. ink
Artworks: Mike Phillips

Picture credits: Age Fotostock/Superstock: 11c; Kelvin
Aitken/Alamy: 11b; Yusef Anil Akduygu/istockphoto: 11b; Richard
Baker/Alamy:27br; Ed Berien/Shutterstock: 11t; Bettmann/Corbis:
7r; Craft Vision/istockphoto: 7b;
Jens Fisbaek/istockphoto: front cover b; Lynn
Graesing/istockphoto: 27bl; Grafissimo/istockphoto: 21b; Denise
Hager/Alamy: 26; Gavin Hellier/Alamy: 19b; John Henshall/Alamy:
7br; www..iwalktoschool.org: 17t;
Jupiter Images/Thinkstock/Alamy: front cover t; Shane
Kato/istockphoto: 15t; Brian Keen/Alamy: 9t; Morgan Lane
Photographers/Shutterstock: 6; Frank Leung/istockphoto: 15b;
René Lorenz/istockphoto: 9b; EGD/Shutterstock: 10; Gary
Martin/istockphoto: 21t; Steven May/Alamy: 24; Ian
Miles/Flashpoint/Alamy: 16; James Morgan/Shutterstock: 8l;
Dmitry Naumov/Shutterstock: 17b;
Lindsey Parnaby/epa/Corbis: 11c; Alex Segre/Alamy: 18b, 20; Joe
Sohm/Alamy: 18t; Ray Tang/Rex Features: 23b;
Peter Titmuss/Alamy: 19t, 22t; Terry Whittaker/Alamy: 25b.

To Jez—maybe stick to walking from now on.

February 2011
RD/6000006415/001

"During 25 years of writing about the environment for the Guardian, *I quickly realized that education was the first step to protecting the planet on which we all depend for survival. While the warning signs are everywhere that the Earth is heating up and the climate changing, many of us have been too preoccupied with living our lives to notice what is going on in our wider environment. It seems to me that it is children who need to know what is happening—they are often more observant of what is going on around them. We need to help them to grow up respecting and preserving the natural world on which their future depends. By teaching them about the importance of water, energy, and other key areas of life, we can be sure they will soon be influencing their parents' lifestyles, too. This is a series of books every child should read."*

Paul Brown

Former environment correspondent
for the UK's *Guardian* newspaper,
environmental author, and fellow of
Wolfson College, Cambridge, UK.

Contents

Words in **bold** can be found in the glossary on page 28.

Getting Around

How did you get to school today? Did you go on a bicycle? Maybe you walked? Many of your class will have traveled by car, some, perhaps, by school bus. It's unlikely that any of you went by plane!

Lots of children travel to school every day on a school bus.

Transportation

As we move from place to place, within our village, town, or city, or between countries, we use different forms of **transportation** to get around. We can choose to walk, cycle, or to go by car, bus, streetcar, boat, train, or plane.

Early Travel

Until the second half of the twentieth century, people did not often travel far. Cars were too expensive for the average family, and air travel was not common. If people did go abroad, they usually went by ship.

After World War I (1914–1918), technology that had been developed for fighter planes was used to improve air travel. In June 1939, there was the first "commercial" flight, for general air travel, from New York to Marseille, in France.

Passengers on the first around-the-world flight, June 30, 1947.

Eating food gives us the energy to move around.

Travel and Energy

All travel uses **energy**. Traveling on foot and cycling use our body's energy. Our energy comes from the food we eat, so we need to make sure that we have breakfast before we set off! All other forms of transportation use fuel, most often **gasoline** or **diesel**, to make them go.

The Rise of the Car

Can you estimate how many cars there are where you live? Does every house have a car parked outside? And how many houses are there near you? Nowadays, most households, particularly those in **developed countries**, have one or more cars.

Developed vs. Developing

The top ten countries for car ownership are all developed countries. In the U.S., more than 140 million people— that's almost half of the total **population**—own a car. In the UK, there are around 31 million cars, and in New Zealand, nearly everyone old enough to drive owns a car! People in **developing countries** are less likely to own a car, because cars are expensive to buy and maintain. But car ownership in developing countries is growing fast.

There are more than four times as many people in China as in the U.S., but in China, there are about nine million cars. In the U.S., however, there are more than 140 million! →

TO THE MOON AND BACK

If all forms of passenger transportation in the United States were lined up, bumper-to-bumper, they would reach from the Earth to the Moon and back. The fuel needed to run all these vehicles for one year would fill a swimming pool the size of a football field and 40 miles (64 km) deep!

It is estimated that by 2031, there will be 33.5 million cars on the roads in the UK. If all these cars were parked at the same time, they would fill a 52-lane freeway from London to Edinburgh. That's about 400 miles (650 km)!

Many people choose to drive to out-of-town shopping centers rather than shop in stores in their local area.

Car Lifestyles

Nowadays, people in developed countries don't often think about how much they rely on their cars to get around. Even the way in which we arrange our towns and cities shows how much we depend on cars. For example, it is now common to have out-of-town shopping centers that you need a car to reach. In some countries, such as Australia and New Zealand, the distances between places are very great. Having a car makes it a lot easier for people to get around.

The longest highway in the world runs almost all the way around Australia and is more than 12,425 miles (20,000 km) long.

Traveling the World

We don't just move around within our countries. Have you heard the expression that the world is now a "global village"? This means that because of modern transportation, it's now so much easier and faster to travel around the world that it feels as though we live in a small village.

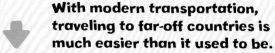
With modern transportation, traveling to far-off countries is much easier than it used to be.

Flying High

The fastest way to travel long distances is by plane. Planes can fly through the skies at more than 560 mph (900 km/h)! There are around 200,000 flights around the world every day. That's more than 8,330 flights every hour, 138 flights every minute, or over two flights a second. It is exhausting even just thinking about it!

Train Travel

To travel shorter distances, many people choose to travel by train. For example, in New York City alone, about 4.8 million people a day travel on subways, using 26 lines from 468 stations. Trains can also travel longer distances, though at a much slower rate than by plane. You can travel under the sea on a train from the UK to France through the Channel Tunnel, or from one sea to another, from the Indian Ocean to the Pacific, across Australia.

It's more than 2,670 miles (4,300 km) from Perth to Sydney by train across Australia's Nullarbor Desert. It takes around three days.

Ship Ahoy!

And it's not just people who move around. Nowadays, goods (the things we buy) are often made in one country and sold in another, so we move goods from one country to another all the time. Things can be moved by ship, or flown by air. Most goods tend to go by ship because this is cheaper. In fact, there are about 50,000 cargo ships from more than 150 countries used to transport goods of all kinds all around the world.

About 90 percent of goods are carried by ship.

Getting Hotter!

All of this travel takes a big toll on our **environment**. The explosion in car and plane journeys in particular has been linked with both **global warming** and **climate change**.

Fossil Fuels

In order to work, cars, most trucks, trains, and planes need gasoline, diesel, and oil. These are known as **fossil fuels**. Fossil fuels are formed under the ground over millions of years.

When fossil fuels are burned, they release energy and this makes cars and other vehicles move. However, when the fuels are burned, they also release a gas called **carbon dioxide** (CO_2).

Global Warming

2. CO_2 is a greenhouse gas, one of the gases in the Earth's **atmosphere** that trap the Sun's heat. As more fuel is used, more greenhouse gases are added to the atmosphere. This means that more heat is kept in, warming the Earth up.

3. Rising temperatures have started to change the weather patterns around the world. This is called climate change.

1. Coal, oil, and gas develop underground over millions of years. When they are burned, they create energy. Burning these fuels gives off carbon dioxide **emissions**.

Global Warming

Earth's climate varies naturally, but evidence shows that people have made it change faster by burning more and more fossil fuels. One effect of this is a gradual increase in the Earth's temperature. Out of the five warmest years on record, four have occurred in the last ten years.

Cracked earth in the U.S. and flooding in the UK show the effects of climate change around the world.

Extreme Weather

We can already see the effects of climate change, with extreme weather patterns forming all around the world. **Heat waves** and **droughts** are becoming more common in some areas, while rainfall can be very heavy in others, causing flooding. Extreme weather events, such as hurricanes, are also increasing around the world.

Did you know?

Driving a car for 3,100 miles (5,000 km) or flying between London and Moscow four times creates one ton of CO_2—the same weight as a fully grown, female walrus.

A Necessary Trip?

Luckily, there is a lot we can all do to help reduce how our journeys affect the environment. First, we can all try to cut down on the number of trips we make by car.

An Elephant a Year

In the United States, the average car releases about 4.6 tons of CO_2 into the air each year. That's nearly an elephant's-worth of CO_2 for every car, every year! American cars and light trucks are responsible for nearly half of all greenhouse gases emitted worldwide. So people who have cars cannot just blame air **pollution** and global warming on other people—they all play a part.

Use It Less!

We need to start thinking about whether we need to use our cars as much as we do. Here are some simple things to think about each time you and your parents or carers are about to get in the car:

Can you:
- save up chores and do them all together to reduce the number of trips?
- share a car trip with a friend or neighbor?
- choose not to go in the car? Is the errand close enough to travel on foot, by bike, or on **public transit**?

 Taking the bus to school is better for the environment than going by car, but walking is even better!

Lighten the Load

Traveling 15 miles (24 km) less each week in our cars would reduce our carbon emissions by 900 pounds (408 kg) a year. That's saving the same weight in CO_2 per person as the weight of two American black bears. Remember, in the U.S., there are more than 62 million cars, so that would save more than 124 million bear's-worth of CO_2 from going into the air each year.

 Imagine if we all saved a couple of bear's-worth of CO_2 each year! That adds up to a big saving.

What About Walking?

One way we can cut down on our car trips is by walking more. Did you know that nearly one-quarter of trips we make by car are shorter than 2 miles (3 km) in distance? That's less than a half-an-hour walk.

The Walking Bus

Would it be possible to walk to school from where you live? Many schools around the world have a "Walking Bus." This is where authorized adults stop at agreed "bus stops" on a well-used route to school, to "pick up" children to walk them to school in a group. Walking is good for you and, as the only fuel you use is your own energy, it's good for the environment too!

In a walking bus like this one, there is always an adult "driver" and some other adult "conductors" to make sure the children are safe.

Walk Around the World

There are international schemes such as WOW—walk to school once a week—that aim to get children walking to school. In October, there is an international walk-to-school program where children from all around the world get together in that week to walk to their school. In 2007, a record 42 countries took part to make it a more "walkable world."

Make sure you have permission from your parent or carer before you go out for a walk.

WONDERS OF WALKING

Walking regularly is a great way to keep your body fit and it is one of the safest forms of exercise. It helps to keep your heart, lungs, and muscles in good condition, it strengthens your bones, and it also helps to control your weight. What's not to like?

On Your Bike

Did you know that for the **natural resources** and energy it takes to make one car, you could make about 100 bicycles? Once it has been made, it is your energy that makes a bicycle work, not the Earth's.

Fit and Planet Friendly

Traveling by bike is a great way to stay in shape. It doesn't put strain on your body, but it gives your heart and muscles a good workout. If you are traveling in a town, it can often be quicker to travel by bike than car because many roads have lanes that only buses and bicycles can use. And the only energy you burn when cycling is your body's, so the only CO_2 emissions from cycling are in the air we breathe out!

A bicycle is 30 times less expensive to buy and keep going than a car.

Trips of less than 5 miles (8 km), and those in busy areas, are often quicker on a bike than in a car.

Did you know?

You can travel up to four times faster on a bicycle than you can by walking, using the same amount of energy.

Cycle Safely

It is very important that you only cycle with your parents or carers. Be sure to wear a cycle helmet that fits properly and ride on a bike that is roadworthy. If you are cycling on or near roads, you should wear the correct reflective clothing so that cars and other vehicles can see you clearly.

Regular cycling is a great way to get in shape and stay active, but make sure you have the correct equipment before you go.

BIKES GALORE

The Netherlands sets a good example of how to encourage more people to cycle. It has spent millions of dollars on developing good cycle paths, with separate traffic signals for bikes. Often, the bike has right of way over other vehicles on the road. The Netherlands has a population of 15 million people, and 12 million of them own bikes!

This bike park is by the main train station in Amsterdam, in the Netherlands.

Go on Public Transit!

Sometimes, it's just not possible to walk or go by bike because we need to travel too far. But don't jump in the car yet! Have you ever thought about riding on public transit?

Bus, Train, or Streetcar

Some of us have gotten so used to relying on our cars that it wouldn't cross our minds to catch a bus or train to go somewhere. Yet there are several advantages to bus travel, besides the fact that it is environmentally friendly and saves you buying gas. If you go by bus you do not have to struggle to find your way around in a new area, and you do not have to search for a parking space or pay big-city parking fees.

Can you give me a ride to the bus stop?

Bad Name

Unfortunately, public transportation can sometimes have a bad name because trains or buses often run late, or are too crowded at rush hour. However, many people think that if more of us use public transportation, and demand that it is run better, it will have to improve.

 U.S. families living near public transit links drive, on average, 4,400 miles (7,080 km) less per year.

Here are some things we can all do to help improve how we use our local public transit:

- get up-to-date timetables for your area; look for special deals, and try to book in advance for a cheaper price
- ask your parent or carer if you can use public transit instead of the car for a few regular trips. Plan them very carefully. Try and make these regular changes to your week's travel
- when public transit is unsatisfactory, write to your local political representative.

Buy train tickets in advance to save money on your fare.

CASE STUDY

GET ON BOARD!

By train, plane, or car? Or bus? Of all these ways to travel, the intercity bus is the most environmentally friendly way to go. This is mainly because buses can carry a lot of people all at once. Research shows that buses release just 2 ounces (0.06 kg) of CO_2 per passenger-mile (every 2 km). This is half what trains give out, and much much smaller than the amount given out by cars and planes. So get on board!

One full intercity bus in the U.S. can take 55 cars off the road.

Reduce Car Use

Sometimes, traveling by car is simply the most convenient and efficient way to get from A to B. But there are ways of making traveling by car more environmentally friendly.

Car Sharing

If your trip to school is too far to walk or cycle, perhaps you could talk to your parents or carers about sharing the car. Do you live near a classmate? Perhaps you could take turns making the trip by car? But remember—your safety comes first. Car sharing should be a proper arrangement made by your parent or carer.

Did you know?

A standard car will produce its own weight in CO_2 once it has done about 6,000 miles (9,600 km)— usually within a year.

SHARE THE STRAIN!

People working for the same company or in the same town or city can join a carpool, where they share their journey details and then team up with someone who lives near them to share rides. To reduce traffic and encourage sharing (also called carpooling) some countries have introduced car-share lanes, as well as reserving parking places especially for carpoolers. Car sharing is a more environmentally friendly and sustainable way to travel by car.

Carpoolers use less gas, spend less, reduce pollution, and even save time because some roads have car-share lanes that are less busy.

Go Eco or Electric

If your family needs a new car, why not choose an eco car or an electric one? Eco cars produce far fewer CO_2 emissions than traditional cars and there are now many models available. Alternatively, you could buy an electric car. Electric cars run on electricity rather than gasoline, and are powered by a rechargeable battery. Electric cars still produce CO_2, however, because fossil fuels are burned to produce the electricity that powers the cars.

Did you know?

The car is the main form of transportation in the U.S., and there are 752 motor vehicles for every 1,000 people.

Some electric cars, like these ones in England, can travel for up to six hours and for about 80 miles (128 km) on one charge.

Planet-Friendly Travel

Air travel is one of the biggest causes of air pollution and makes a big contribution to global warming. With more than 200,000 flights a day worldwide and an average plane using 1 gallon (4 l) of fuel per second, it's not hard to see why. So it's important to think about different ways of traveling long distances when possible.

Flying Facts

Each day, there are about 1.8 million passengers in the sky over the U.S. on one of the 24,600 flights that travel over America.

All models of the Boeing 747 plane have traveled about 50 billion miles (80.4 billion km); that's the same as flying to the Moon and back 75,000 times.

Greener Vacations

It is important that all of us, wherever we live, think carefully about how we can reduce our impact on the environment when we go on vacation. There are things that we can all do:

- take our vacations within our own state to avoid flying or traveling far
- look into all the ways to travel, by train, boat, or bus to see which is most environmentally friendly
- use travel companies that are eco-friendly.

 You don't have to travel far to have a really great vacation.

Carbon Offsetting

We all have a carbon footprint. A carbon footprint trail is an imaginary trail that we leave when we use electricity, oil, and gas in our homes, schools, and workplaces, and fuel in our vehicles. Every time we use a "carbon" energy (coal, oil, or gas), it gives off CO_2. Organizations that have a large carbon footprint, such as big companies, can "offset" this carbon by helping to look after the environment. They can do this by donating money or "carbon credits" to organizations that carry out projects all over the world to reduce the amount of CO_2 that goes into the air.

We each have a carbon footprint. It is measured in tons of CO_2 released into the air.

Carbon credits can be put toward funding environmental projects such as wind farms, a source of "clean," renewable energy.

Going the Distance

To change how we travel, we must first change our habits. We can start simply, by changing just one trip we make each week. If we keep it simple, we are more likely to make the change last.

Walk into the Record Books

Many of us can walk to school. Find out when the international walk to school month is, and help take it into the record books by joining the millions of people who are already taking part. Who knows? Walking to school may become another good habit! And it will keep you in shape as well as being good for the environment.

Small things can add up to make big ones. If we all make one trip less by car a week and walk or cycle instead, that adds up to a lot less CO_2 going into the air.

FUTURE FUELS

We are never going to stop traveling completely, so scientists are developing new types of fuel.

Green electricity, sourced through renewable energies such as wind, solar, and tidal power, will provide more of our electricity in the future. This will make the electric car a much greener type of transportation.

Biofuels are an alternative fuel to gasoline. They are made from plants that are burned to produce energy. They cancel out the CO_2 they make when they are burned by using up CO_2 as they grow. However, some people think that biofuels use up land that should be used to grow food, and that biofuels create different types of pollution.

Another form of energy is hydrogen fuel cells. This is where the chemicals hydrogen and oxygen are combined in the fuel cell into water, producing electricity. This electricity can be used as power, instead of gasoline, for example.

Plug in to recharge and then take off!

This plant makes biofuel from grain.

Glossary

Atmosphere The layer of gases that surround the Earth.

Biofuels Fuels made from plant matter.

Carbon dioxide A gas in the air.

Carpool An arrangement when people who work together or live nearby share their cars to get around.

Climate change Long-term changes to the world's weather patterns.

Developed countries Countries with highly developed economies, where most of the population work in factories and businesses.

Developing countries Countries with less developed economies, where most of the population work in farming.

Diesel A fuel made from oil that is used to power cars and other vehicles.

Drought A shortage of rain over a long period of time.

Emissions Substances, such as the gas carbon dioxide, that escape into the air.

Energy The power to make or do something.

Environment Surroundings.

Fossil fuels Fuel such as coal, oil, or gas, that have developed under the ground from rotting animal and plant life over millions of years.

Gasoline A fuel made from oil.

Global warming The gradual heating up of the Earth's atmosphere.

Heat wave Unusually hot weather in an area over a long period of time.

Natural resources Materials, such as water and wood, that are found in nature.

Pollution Making something, such as the air or water, dirty.

Population The number of people living in a place.

Public transit A system of vehicles, such as trains, streetcars, subways, and buses, that follow set routes at set times for people to use to travel from one place to another by paying a fare.

Renewable Something that is in constant supply and will not run out, such as the wind.

Tidal power A type of energy produced by harnessing the power of the tides of the sea.

Transportation Different types of vehicles, such as cars, buses, airplanes, and so on, used for carrying people or goods from one place to another.

Useful Information

Throughout this book, "real-life measurements" are used for reference. These measurements are not exact, but give a sense of just how much an amount is, or what it looks like.

Walrus = 1 TON

Asian elephant = 5 TONS

American black bear = 440 POUNDS (200 KG)

Cirumference at Equator = 25,000 MILES (40,000 KM)

Earth to the Moon Average Distance = 239,000 MILES (384,500 KM)

Further reading

Earthwise: Getting Around by Jim Pipe (Franklin Watts, 2008)

Action for the Environment: Transport Solutions by A. Gilpin (Franklin Watts, 2006)

Web Sites

www.ctc.org.uk
The web site for the International Walk to School organization.

www.bikeleague.org
The web site of the League of American Bicyclists, which promotes bicycling for fun, fitness, and transportation.

www.care2.com/channels/ecoinfo/ transportation
Lists web sites for young environmentalists with information about transportation, including hybrid cars, and the environment.

Dates to Remember

Earth Hour—March 28

Earth Day—April 22

World Environment Day—June 5

Clean Air Day—June

Walk to School Campaign—May and October

World Food Day—October 16

America Recycles Day—November 15

Note to parents and teachers: Every effort has been made by the Publishers to ensure that these web sites are suitable for children, that they are of the highest educational value, and that they contain no inappropriate or offensive material. However, because of the nature of the Internet, it is impossible to guarantee that the contents of these sites will not be altered. We strongly advise that Internet access is supervised by a responsible adult.

Index